WALKING WITH GOD

*How to Best Enjoy
Jesus as Lord*

The Full Picture

Michael J Spyker

AgapeDeum

Published in Adelaide, Australia by AgapeDeum
Contact: agapedeum.com

ISBN 978-0-6455379-0-1

Copyright © Michael J Spyker 2022

All right reserved. Other than for the purpose and subject to the conditions prescribed under the *Copyright Act*, no part of this publication may be reproduced, stored in a retrieval system, or transmitted in any form or by any means, electronic, mechanical, photocopying, recording and otherwise, without prior permission of the publisher.

Publication assistance by Immortalise

    Cover design: Ben Morton

Cover photo by Robert Thiemann on Unsplash

*God is our refuge and strength
A well proved strength in trouble.
Psalm 46:1*

*By the Heart does
Our Deliverance come.*

CONTENT

1.	The Full Picture	1
2.	Come!	4
3.	Personhood	7
4.	Doing Well	10
5.	Redemption	14
6.	Between the Lines	17
7.	In Relation	21
8.	Spirituality	24
9.	Religion	27
10.	God	31
11.	Creation	35
12.	The Cross	38
13.	A Second Birth	41
14.	A New Creation	44
15.	A Greater Reality	47
16.	Standing Strong	51
17.	Scripture	54
18.	Living Waters	58
19.	Heaven	61
20.	Meaning	65

1

The Full Picture

Most Christians discover the reality of God in bits and pieces as they go to church. Those pieces are selective and coloured by the kind of church they are attending. Not often is the full picture of God's involvement with our world given and when it is, the information can become overly academic. A concise presentation in easy language that is also comprehensive, is not that readily found.

Often believers are quite happy with just the pieces they know about. They may not even realise that those pieces make not the complete puzzle. Christian life with a limited picture of God is quite liveable. But it can lack a good understanding of Jesus as Lord. The truly spiritual Christian will arrive at this understanding by spending quality time with Jesus. Yet even then, being aware of the full picture will be beneficial.

Engaging in religion can be both invigorating and unnerving. It may lift the spirit but can present difficulties that have little to do with God also; troubles of a distinctly human nature. How to deal with such situations needs discernment. An adequate idea of what the picture of God looks like offers a frame of reference suitable in dealing with church matters and equally so with life in general.

Understanding God needs information and putting the pieces together. Besides using the intellect however, a commitment of the heart is required to bring the idea of God alive. It is a spiritual matter and important, for unless the sprit is stirred, the Lord cannot be enjoyed and life will not change for the better which, after all, should be what Christianity is all about. A meaningful Christian life seeks to make the full picture of God shine vibrantly.

I have written a number of books over the years always with Jesus in mind and urging towards a recognition of his supremacy. Various insights from spiritual theology, philosophy, psychology, religion and the sciences were used in making my case. It was a journey in understanding with the writing process demanding a proper formulation of ideas that at times presented matters a little differently from the norm but were always orthodox. It focused on God, creation and people. Now I would like to present the important insights of my study in a concise and easy to read way leaving the academic side alone though every idea is gained from that knowledge. For half a century now I have walked with God in the footsteps of Enoch (Gen. 5:24) and it seemed a good title for this little book.

We live in a world that overflows with messages. Today's news is tomorrow's history and that approach presents a problem. Spending quality time with information is no longer common and this lack of focused attention can be detrimental to the spiritual life. Christian wellbeing will only prosper in its full potential when spending time with the Lord and reflecting on what God really is about. The topics to follow have been selected to offer a fairly wide spectrum of what counts most when engaging with God, ourselves, people and church; the information needed for a full picture.

You will find ideas that are familiar, but maybe are being explained a little differently. Also ideas that may be unfamiliar, but make sense and will help towards a greater appreciation of the Lord and the divine plan. Enjoy the read, and whatever strikes you as important, please take it to heart.

2

Come!

Such a simple word 'come'. And yet it is the key to understanding God. It is a relational word and with God a matter of spirit and heart for only then will the divine become real. I am invited to simply come into a personal relationship with Jesus and the many benefits that brings.

Any suggestion that God remains at a distance from people is false. The Lord is closer than breathing and when Jesus invites to come there are no barriers. Nothing will ever prevent me from reaching him but my own reservations. Such as: ideas that there are certain ways by which to come, or that I should get myself a bit sorted first. Thoughts like that are irrelevant to God. Scripture states that I find my existence in the Son, that my soul originates from him and finds life in him 24/7 (Col. 1:15). I find my life in a God who *is* Love. Love of a magnitude I cannot imagine and of a power I cannot escape from. Jesus is ever present and readily found.

Of course, believing all this to be true is a matter of

faith. Only believing will open the door to divine reality, which applies to any kind of worship ever practised by humanity. You have to believe in what you spiritually seek to engage with. Religious faith often uses elaborate rites and rituals in approaching the transcendent and it is no different for Christianity. Fortunately, such techniques are not essential in connecting with God and may well become a hindrance when they take prominence while their function should be to facilitate engagement of the believer with the divine. *God is not religious but relational.* God relates Person to person without an intermediary.

When Jesus says 'come' my response is an action from the heart that simply accepts the invitation. Jesus will be attentive to it and a relational communication begins. It may not feel that way, but it does. Come, simply means come; no provisos or techniques apply. The scope and possibilities of the invitation are given in the Gospel of Matthew. Jesus was upbraiding the unbelief of Israel's religious leadership and the unnecessary burdens they imposed upon their people. The Lord frequently was a loggerheads with religion and told his hearers what it would mean to follow him instead.

Come to me, all who labour and are heavy laden, and

> I will give you rest. Take my yoke upon you, and learn from me; for I am gentle and lowly in heart, and you will find rest for your souls. For my yoke is easy and my burden is light (Matt. 11:28-30).

That call rings just as clearly today. I have taken heed of it throughout my Christian life with many benefits, both immediate when restoring the equilibrium in my soul and long-term by finding the Lord's wisdom being increased in my spirit. I have come to understand the Lord much better. It is a mysterious but real process. God wouldn't be much of a god, if it didn't involve mystery and I take pleasure from recognising it happening in my life. I make sure to 'come' every day.

3

Personhood

People are the crown of God's creation and are able to experience and express the nature and attributes of God to a measure. They can love, live good lives and are mentally capable. Unfortunately, people are exposed to totally opposite qualities also, those engendered by sin.

Life is experienced in a material body enlivened by spirit. Body and spirit are so completely integrated into one that their division is impossible. Only at death will the spirit of a person return to God while the material body disintegrates into the earth (Eccl. 12:7). Spirit and body interact and when this results into an awareness, I consider it to be the experience of soul.

Many of God's creatures are aware and thus have a soul. Personhood is special in that unlike other living beings its awareness is deliberate rather than instinctive and is endowed with the knowledge of good and evil. Furthermore, personhood so much carries the image of God that Jesus, the Son of God, could become a person without thereby violating his essential nature though he entered a much diminished mode of being (Phil. 2:5-7). Such is the magnitude of personhood.

It is in my soul that I feel how life is treating me and when Jesus invites me to come he offers rest for my soul. Partly it can be immediate in that I may feel more restful in spirit. A more deeply anchored rest will take time and is a learning experience with the Lord as my teacher. It is a subtle process and not readily defined. Much of the learning is spiritual with my spirit being encouraged and empowered towards what is good for me. Wellbeing depends much on the state of a person's soul and it is thought that about 80% of illness has a psychosomatic component. An active relationship with Jesus settles the emotions and is good for psycho-spiritual health.

My disposition of soul determines much and colours my relationship with people and also the Lord. I can be my own worst enemy. In growing up I have been exposed to pressures, both with family and also culturally. My ego struggled and may have taken on negative tendencies such as selfishness, chips on shoulders and entrenched opinions. Pride can become a problem or convictions of superiority. None of this bears well for the soul. Every person has some attitudes that are best unlearned. Every person also is capable of much good.

The challenge is whether I am willing to have my disposition of soul transformed for it to better align with the Lord's spirit. Do I have the desire to learn from him and improve soul health? Improving life in accordance with divine wisdom has many benefits. It is not tiresome but uplifting. It takes effort but is not exhausting. Jesus tells me that his yoke is easy and his burden is light.

Christian identity formation is a slow process, little steps to take at a time as guided by the Holy Spirit. Central to succeeding well is what Jesus describes about himself, that he is lowly in heart – in other words: humble. It is a disposition of spirit that develops almost naturally once we understanding well the tender love of the Lord. With that insight personhood will flourish. Only humble people will ever be truly free for they have been liberated from unhelpful dictates of their sinful self. It is what Jesus alluded to when declaring, 'If the Son makes you free, you will be free indeed' (John 8:36). The wellbeing of personhood depends on disposition of spirit and soul; on allowing the Lord to bring about wholeness. Jesus' statement about becoming free referred to him defeating sin on the cross also and to setting people free from sin forever. Personhood is eternal.

4

Doing Well

With people being so special and able to distinguish between good and evil, it stands to reason that this capacity counts heavily in the eyes of God. It is made clear early in the Bible with the story of Cain and Abel. When Cain's offering is rejected, and not Abel's, God explains the situation to Cain and introduces a theme that runs throughout Scripture.

> Why are you angry, and why has your countenance fallen? If you do well, will you not be accepted? And if you do not well, sin is couching at the door; its desire is for you, but you must master it (Gen. 4:7).

Seek to do well or sin will jump at you, is the advice. Live a good life and God will be pleased. It is the spiritual reality of every person. Scripture insists that good living will find its blessings and even an eternal reward. All that is good reflects the nature of God and will not go unnoticed by the Lord. Within personhood doing well finds opposition however, which I must withstand in my spirit and mind. It is a constant problem highlighted by Apostle Paul's frustrations. He explained that there is a negative power working within him that prevents living up to his desired standard. It is inescapable and finds its origin in the influences of sin (Rom. 7:21-25). Paul was referring to the basic tendencies of sinfulness that are integrated within every single person from birth. Its manifestations are many such as selfishness, not looking after myself, being grumpy and the like. Generally, God holds nobody accountable for that. I must try to do right as best I can and inevitable mistakes are forgiven.

Not so when sinful tendencies become evil, when morally questionable choices are wilfully made and I enter Cain's dilemma. I must master the temptation towards doing wrong, call on the Lord's help, and make sure to stay on the straight and narrow. Cain did quite the opposite when soon after God's warning he murdered his brother Abel. God's response was swift. Life for Cain was to become very difficult. He would become a fugitive and wander the earth. Cain was devastated and exclaimed, 'whoever finds me will slay me.' Not so, God said and put a mark on Cain that stopped him from being killed (Gen. 4:8-16).

Figuratively, this story portrays the workings of evil in the human psyche; how sin will unravel wellbeing. The power of sin, however, cannot steal a life away for all of life is eternally God's. Sin destroys by disintegration while from God issues life and the good, which is the divine purpose. People are expected to do right and are able to. It is this ability of wilful choice that sets people apart in a natural world that lives by instinct. Every person faces Cain's dilemma, 'Do well and will you not be accepted?' An honourable life counts for much in the eyes of God.

Throughout Scripture the theme of right living appears and it features consistently in Apostle Paul's letters. Put to death, he tells the believers in Colossae: anger, wrath, malice, slander and foul talk. Rather, put on: compassion, kindness, lowliness, meekness and patience (Col. 3:5-17). In other letters by Paul the range of pros and cons is expanded. It was the negative tendencies in people he had the most problems with in guiding the churches. Little has changed in this regard.

Doing well is of central importance in life. It is an ability that resides in the human spirit and in cognitive capacity. God is serious about morality whether a person is Christian or not. People who are unaware of God and live morally right will find the Lord's acceptance as their conscience will stand up to divine scrutiny (Rom. 2:14-16). In the eyes of God doing well is more important than being 'spiritual' whatever one's creed.

It is good to know that as a Christian I can affirm my belief daily by the ordinary; by living like a decent person before the Lord. I understand that the value of my religious sentiments is much determined by the nature of my soul – by its disposition. Wrong attitudes will diminish the spiritual quality of personhood.

5

Redemption

The world is an expression of God's Love and exists in Christ. This statement is true but needs to be accepted by faith. In our world love and peace seem to be in short supply while creation finding its being in Jesus cannot be scientifically verified. It has to be taken at faith value.

Clearly, our world suffers under a destructive power, the power of sin. It is sin for the reason that it is not God. Scripture tells me that sin is here to stay until God makes all things new and it will no longer have legitimacy. This has been the divine plan from before the creation of the universe: that all will be restored into perfection, into a new reality with a beauty and magnitude that is beyond imagination. An eternal reality that is a haven of love and joy. It has been preordained and will happen as the Son of God has redeemed all that sin has ruined.

Apart from doing well and good living, redemption is the second major theme that runs throughout Scripture. The creation story in Genesis 1 tells us that all God created was very good. Still today, all that is good on earth reflects the nature of God. Genesis 2 introduces the problem of sin, a force of destruction and disintegration. It brought death into the world. Fortunately, God made sure that death is not the end but actually an escape for all of creation away from sin into a better future. Jesus Christ would make that possible as foretold in Genesis.

In the creation story the serpent is instrumental in bringing sin into the world. One day its head would be crushed by someone born of a woman (Gen. 3:14-15). The power of sin was not to last forever. Creation would be redeemed, bought back with a price, from the clutches of sin. In the Old Testament the arrival of a Messiah, a deliverer, is often alluded to. However, the nature of that delivery and the kind of person bringing it about became misunderstood. When at last the Christ arrived, he ended up condemned on a cross.

The Son himself, in whom all exists, became the sacrifice to set all of creation free – past, present and future. All that ever was, has been redeemed, rescued at a terrible cost – the life of the Son. Were not everything redeemed, sin would have been able to extract some of what exists in Christ away from the Godhead. That cannot be, for his victory over sin is utterly complete.

The victory was a divine one and reached into the realm of the Trinity to stop any legitimacy sin may have had in infiltrating creation. Therefore, Apostle Paul could write: 'the creation itself will be set free from its bondage to decay and obtain the glorious liberty of the children of God' (Rom. 8 21).

Already now that liberty dwells actively within those who have genuinely asked the spirit of Jesus to dwell within their being as a promise of an eternal sin-free future. That Christ's victory is universal Paul confirms in 1 Timothy 4:10. 'For we have our hope set on the living God, who is the Saviour of everyone, especially those who believe.'

Paul making the statement, 'especially those who believe,' is interesting. I interpret it to mean that those who have 'come' to Jesus by faith find themselves in a privileged position. They may already now benefit from a special influence: a holy spirit that resides within their being. The very spirit whereby God's New Creation has come to exists. Within the believer that new spirit is now fully integrated with that person's spirit, body and soul. It has many benefits and is a mystery.

6

Between the Lines

Life is never easy and people tend to cope as best they can. There are so many dynamics involved with being a person. I have a body and a spirit. I am conscious, can think and feel. My five senses enrich life while having a will makes choices possible. I am a relational being who lives with other people, animals and birds, while society seeks to impart its cultural norms. All that, while I develop from year to year into the person I presently am. So many influences to deal with and I am expected to do okay in it all. Add to it the insights and demands of Christian living and the challenge becomes a heady mix. Into this Jesus says 'come' and promises proficiency.

After becoming a Christian long ago I soon decided that in making good sense of my existence I needed to understand the Lord as best I could as it is he who gives life. And so the walk began over many years in which I have consulted the Lord in my spirit. Being by nature analytical I sought an approach to my understanding that was systematic and supportive of spiritual knowing. My mind in support of my heart.

I soon discovered how little I was able to know about God's reality, but what I could know has proven to be more than sufficient. There is a realm which I have called 'unknowing'. Understanding this realm is beyond me and any information revealed by it needs to be taken by faith, intuition and acceptance.

Besides 'unknowing' there is ever the danger of sin and it can become my 'undoing'. I face that problem consistently. Both unknowing and undoing are very real to me. They are important in my Christian life and I visualise it with a mental picture.

Draw a stick figure with a horizontal line above it and one beneath it. Above the top line write 'unknowing' and beneath the bottom line write 'undoing'. That is how I see myself. In between those lines the stick figure makes the best of life seeking to do right with Jesus as a friend. But the two lines represent dynamic realities and have their particular influences.

The challenges of 'undoing' are twofold. Firstly, what Paul spoke about calling himself wretched when finding within himself urges that countered what he mentally set out to achieve (Rom. 7:21-25). The daily battle between living sort of perfectly and making mistakes. In addition, undoing involves dangers that are truly harmful to the soul – wilful and serious wrongdoing that borders or enters the realms of evil. It surely must be avoided.

Likewise, the realm of 'unknowing' has two sides to it. Firstly, there are the many statements about divine reality which I cannot comprehend. That everything exists in Jesus Christ, as enormous as the universe, is a statement I simply cannot get my head around. Nor that God knows every person on earth, the billions of them, individually. It all has to be accepted by faith. Then secondly, there is a spiritual tradition of unknowing in Christianity that suggest a coming to Jesus that leaves your mind in a blank so that thoughts will not interfere with what the Lord might wish to convey to spiritual perception. A blank mind is not readily achieved and I have found that simply focussing in quiet reflection upon God, while nipping thoughts that are irrelevant in the bud, works fine. But the idea of rather not thinking at all, a blank mind, will linger.

While in reflection, a sense of the presence of Jesus may arrive, perhaps with impressions and insights that are unforeseen. I may come to rest, the uncomplicated me before the Lord – the essential me, fully known and deeply loved.

The realm of 'unknowing' is interesting in both of its aspects: those facts about God that are mindboggling, or intuitive reflection that bring insights by leaving thoughts behind. God's handiwork and being are too wonderful for me, but I enjoy its mystery. I am happy to enquire a little into what I don't much understand about creation, while avoiding questions that will find no answer. As far as spiritual unknowing is concerned: I am not a mystic. My reflective approach to God is sufficient and more often than not brings a fine experience.

The line of unknowing above my head is not a problem to me. Unlike the line of undoing beneath my feet. I well understand its pitfalls and will remain alert. The little stick figure in my mental picture finds plenty to be busy with between the lines. Mystery hovers above and temptation pulls down below. But the little figure is content.

7

In Relation

We live in a relational universe. Everything, from the largest to the minute in quantum, influences everything else. The sciences recognise it and philosophy also, with a number of theories that focus on the relational as the primary force in creation. It makes sense for God *is* Love, the ultimate positive relational force, and God would not create but in accordance with the divine nature.

God is also Spirit. Love and Spirit are that in which creation finds it existence. Creation is an expression of those two primary dynamics. Sin, which is also relational, is a parasite that feeds on God's handiwork destructively.

As a person, who reflects the nature of God, I have come to understand the relational as very important and I live with that knowledge always in the forefront of my mind. A positive, caring attitude towards everything is of paramount importance and reflects what the Lord is like. .My relational disposition, more than anything else, reveals who I really am. I might hide my true nature from others with affirmative, but false, interactions, but it will not fool God. A genuinely caring person will never even consider such behaviour.

Good relating can be emotionally taxing and perfection is not possible. God fully understands and always looks at the heart rather than shortcomings. Unfortunately, the importance of good relating is often not recognised; that the relational hits at the core of another person's being. Serious troubles are often relational in origin. Something has gone badly wrong because of relational shortcomings. That ranges from wars to troubled families and problems at work.

Relating is an expression of spirit that comes from deep within. Relational disposition determines much. I consider three dynamics as most fundamental towards *positive* relating. I must seek to *care*, to be *responsible* and have *integrity*. Those are key to a good relational attitude. The *negatives* to avoid are: being *authoritarian*, practising *neglect* and using *manipulation*. Negatives like that have a detrimental effect on who is exposed to such behaviour and particularly so with children and teenagers. It leaves a relational imprint that restricts emotional well-being and which they may never fully shake off.

Good relating expresses the nature of love, while the

opposite originates from sinful inclinations. The three positives reside within the nature of Trinity and likewise apply to personhood. I must care, be responsible and have integrity at all times.

I must apply these qualities not just with others but also in my own self-talk. Might I be destructive towards myself and not care because of disappointment or low self-esteem? Am I prone to not being responsible enough with regards to what makes for healthy living? I might fool myself about the reality of things and lack integrity. So much to consider for relating involves almost all that keeps me busy.

Relating is a challenge and the standards of God are high for they reflect the nature of God. But Jesus is not a hard taskmaster, fully knows my difficulties, and will help with the empowerment of grace. He guides and supports me in mysterious ways. The relational is important and I often check my heart about it. I will do my best and will cut myself some slack. A little self-love never goes astray.

8

Spirituality

Years ago, before it became much better known, I was introduced to the Christian tradition of spirituality. It is thousands of years old and offers all that is popular and available from other religions. I had an introduction to Christian spirituality called *Meeting Emma* published in the UK, taught the topic at a theological college and have made spiritual theology my preferred discipline ever since. It never stops to enthuse me.

Christian spirituality encourages to engage with God using proven techniques like spiritual reading, meditation, contemplation, detachment, holy leisure, the Jesus Prayer and more. These methods are of value in focusing the spirit and calming the soul. A fuller understanding of where such a spiritual engagement might lead can be gained from reading books on spirituality and the mystics. It is interesting and enlightening but is not essential to a healthy spiritual soul. A frequent interaction with the Lord is what is mostly required.

I am no mystic and not called to such a pursuit either. I simply live in the conviction that the Lord is continually present in my life. I have 'come' and learned from him, in which the Christian spiritual tradition and its practices have been a great help. I would encourage any believer to become better acquainted with those practices and use techniques towards 'coming to rest' a little in a busy, invasive world.

Spirituality involves the spirit and is relational, for spirit and relation are inseparable, two sides of the same coin. I hold that someone's relational disposition is central to the nature of that person's spirit. An evaluation of someone's spirituality cannot be made without taking that person's relationality into account. Thus Apostle Paul could write, 'If I have not love, I am but a clanging cymbal' (1 Cor. 13:1). The relational determines much and ideally should remain at the forefront of anyone's mind.

In my view, with every person having a spirit and being relational, they have a spirituality of some kind. It may not be religious, but it is their spirit being expressed and projected relationally. Accordingly I see everyone as a spiritual person by nature, as also the Lord does. When religion becomes involved in someone's life it simply adds to the scope of that person's identity and experience.

A religious person would be considered more 'spiritual' than a non-believer but it is a matter of perspective. When religion does little in improving the quality of a believer's relationality, I suggest that a deeply caring non-religious person is more 'spiritual' in expressing the nature of God than an egocentric Christian.

An active involvement in the Christian spiritual tradition can be beneficial towards personal growth. I have found much benefit from it, particularly also in understanding how the 'spirit' dynamics in a person are operative and the possibilities of enlarging the soul. None of this though overshadows the fact that a simple and genuine coming to Jesus without a technique will be equally beneficial. It is what I mostly practise. The Lord needs no methods by which to be approached. He is always and immediately present.

9

Religion

Religion is a construct that establishes and maintains a belief structure in a community. Its leadership oversees its teachings, rites, rituals and holy days, while recording its history. Beliefs and their interpretation tend to become modified over time in accordance with the preference of religious leaders and also societal pressures. Communal cohesion is always in flux. When a religion becomes widely accepted there will be groups within it that begin to dogmatically disagree and sub-groups may eventuate. In Christianity those are called denominations or sects.

God recognises the need in people for religion and instructed Moses in great detail how to set up a mode of worship for Israel with a Tabernacle (tent), a priesthood and laws guarding behaviour. The Tabernacle eventually became replaced by a Temple in Jerusalem. Throughout its history Israel was confronted with Prophets when its people drifted away from God's instructions; when the priesthood had become lax in guiding the community properly. Religion has had its problems throughout the ages.

When Abraham, the founding father of the people of Israel, was called by God, it was a simple encounter. It is not recorded that Abraham ever prayed, but he understood God's intentions and promises perfectly even though those might beggar belief. Abraham trusted God and it was accounted to him as righteousness, Apostle Paul explained many years later. He wished to show that a justification by faith in Jesus Christ likewise makes a Christian enter into a relationship with God without the need of religion (Rom. 4:3-5). It is not religious laws that justify a believer, but trusting in that what God offers in Christ is true and can be spiritually and practically acted upon.

Religion has always been a problem. Jesus, for one, railed against its failures. With its leadership resting on the shoulders of human beings, the history of Christianity is littered with events that are completely opposite to what a loving God is about. Wars and persecutions in the name of religion are well known. The shameful acts of religious leaders are regularly reported these days giving people good reason to avoid church. The Church has lost the trust of many.

Coming to Jesus is like Abraham's engagement with God. It is uncomplicated, not religious, and is personal. God is not religious but relational. Church is meant to facilitate a meaningful interaction between God and the believer, Person to person. It is possible though for the focus to be mostly on rituals and programs instead, with God presumed present in a kind of general way. Rituals and symbols may assist in opening the human spirit to a sense of the transcendent, but they should be portals to Jesus and not an end in themselves.

Christianity has done much good and it continues today. Church is the place to learn about God while Christian community involvement has many benefits. Church can become a place of hurt and disappointment as well. It is to be expected for whenever a group of people come together usually problems arise. Many believers have left church disillusioned and it continues today. But God has not left them and never will. They may reach out to the Lord all the same and will be welcomed.

When Jesus says 'come', this invitation does not depend on church. He was actually making the call while being upset that in spite of his many miracles Israel's spiritual leadership refused his message about the Father (Matt. 11:28-39). What Jesus spoke about did not fit the religious perceptions and purposes of the day and thus the people remained unnecessarily burdened. Jesus was offering an uncomplicated but profound way into God's presence. It is no different now. 'Come' is not a religious call. It is relational and personal without intermediary and offered to all. In the morning of every day Jesus invites me to come and I do so gladly.

10

God

The existence of God cannot be proven or disproven using the power of reason. Many have tried and failed. In the end the question of God's existence is answered by what someone wishes to believe. It makes sense for God is Spirit and it defies mental ability. God is Spirit and Love which are non-substantial influences that may be detected but cannot be measured. Their existence is confirmed by human experience. These days, neurology seeks to make experiences a matter of brain function and no more – a material rather than a spiritual phenomenon. This idea is often disputed as nobody knows where consciousness originates from nor sentience. Modern philosophers, like Colin McGinn in his book *The Mysterious Flame*, are of the opinion that we will not be able to solve that puzzle. There is more to people than bodily function.

The existence of God manifests in the divine handiwork. Apostle Paul wrote: 'Ever since the creation of the world his invisible nature, namely his eternal power and deity, has been clearly perceived in the things that have been made' (Rom. 1:20). A conviction of God being real may be felt in a person's spirit without observing nature also. How that is possible remains a mystery.

A sense of mystery envelopes any deity people may find to worship. The One God of Christianity has many mysteries, but the nature of God has been revealed and God's history with our world has been recorded. The divine plan towards an eternal future for creation is known. God is no stranger; less so since Jesus walked the earth.

Often, when reflecting on the reality of God, I enter into unknowing. So many facts that need to be taken at faith value. I am comfortable with it. Nevertheless, there is no harm in trying to make some reasonable sense of human existence and creation in the care of a divine presence. Theology and philosophy are right in seeking better understanding, as do the sciences. I have taken pleasure in reflecting on God, creation and people and gained a few insights. I am reminded though of what the Preacher concluded. 'For in much wisdom is much vexation, and he who increases in knowledge increases in sorrow' (Eccl. 1:18). It is sage advice. The more you discover the less you seem to know, while wisdom revealing how things ideally should be, can often be troublesome. Still, seeking wisdom and knowledge are worthy exploits.

In understanding God a single realisation overrides all: God *is* Love. It is impossible to know how big a love resides in God. It is massive; way beyond what people feel love to be. With regard to the magnitude of God's love the line of unknowing is quickly reached. Once this line was briefly crossed by me in a vision when the Lord allowed a little insight into the measure of his love. It totally floored me and ever since I have made love the centre of my understanding. God *is* Love and loves me – the whole cosmos exists in love.

God *is* Love and negative emotions are foreign to the divine nature. Medieval mystic Lady Julian of Norwich (1342-1423) saw that there is no anger in God and that makes sense. The sermon by Jonathan Edwards, 'Sinners in the hands of an angry God,' would have been appropriate for the culture of the day as the response it elicited towards repentance showed. Nevertheless, it presents an incorrect idea what God is like. God is never angry with anyone or anything. A better word than anger would be 'indignant'. When God is recorded to have said,

'Jacob I loved, but Esau I hated' (Rom. 9:13), that sentiment is readily understood in its intention. A better linguistic description would be that God 'abhors' what Esau stood for rather than ascribing to God the emotion of hate. Love cannot hate! Words are important and with regard to the nature of God particularly so. The wrong ideas of what God is like have done considerable harm to how believers might feel to approach the divine presence and relate to it.

I much appreciate Julian of Norwich and her account of the Lord's visitations when she was very sick. What she came to understand about Jesus is phenomenal. Nowhere has the nature of the Lord been better revealed. In chapter 72 of her book *Showings* (Revelations) she write that, 'our Lord God dwells now in us, and is here with us, and embraces us and encloses us for his tender love, so that he can never leave us, and is nearer to us than tongue can tell or heart can think.'

I may step into the Lord's presence and have faith in the incredible. God is like that.

11

Creation

Before creation came about its beginning and end were known and planned by God. In its wisdom the Trinity decided that the Father would create in and through Jesus Christ, the Son, by the power of the Holy Spirit (John 1:1-4). God was aware that for reasons unknown to us sin would infiltrate with its destructive powers that which had been created very good. The Trinity accepted it as an unavoidable evil in the knowledge that sin could be defeated one day. A new creation would follow, one that is perfect and eternal.

God is Spirit and God is Love. These are the two forces by which creation exists. Spirit is the primary 'energy' behind everything, while the 'nature' of this energy is Love. Mystics from all major religions have recognised that love is the underlying reality of creation. While modern science and quantum theory reach into the non-substantial and recognise that there is a force behind everything which defies definition. Taking a Christian point of view there is no reason why this force couldn't be Spirit.

From eternal Spirit and eternal Love a creation issues that exists in universal spirit and universal love. There is no divine demarcation between the eternal and universal as creation finds its reality *in* Christ, who is a member of the Trinity. Eternal Love will never disassociate from universal love as it would deny the very nature of Love. Even sin and its terrible power will not be able to drive a wedge between those two expressions of love.

Within creation the power of God's love manifests in all that is good. Every bit of good is a reflection of love's presence. Likewise, all that has life receives this from spirit and love. Sin brings destruction and death into what is living, but its power is temporary and the days are numbered. Creation is a divine work in progress, its scope is beyond imagination, but the storyline is not and has been revealed. Out of nothing the Trinity birthed a perfect creation that became infected with sin. One day that creation will be perfect and without sin.

With our world in much trouble and suffering everywhere the obvious question arises as to why it has to be this way. Julian of Norwich suggests that our present predicament will enable us to better appreciate who God is by nature once we are in heaven. Jesus told her, 'sin is necessary' and she felt not to inquire any further (Chap. 27). Julian understood that once with the Lord in heaven, the reason for sin's existence would be explained to our satisfaction. She also saw that one day God will do a great deed and make all things well!

All I can do is accept it by faith and trust in a good God. My head is bumping against that line of unknowing once again. Julian's views make sense but understanding the deep reason of God in it all is beyond me. All I know is that Jesus paid a very high price in rescuing creation towards an incredible future and I am part of that. It is sufficient.

12

The Cross

The death of Christ was a divine happening that affected the Trinity beyond our imagination. This death was pre-planned before the universe ever came to exist. Christ, in whom everything was created, would redeem a divine handiwork that was destined to fall into destruction because of the power of sin. The divine task was for love to disempower sin at its most primary level. Both are awesome powers without substance that determine the functioning of creation. What needed defeating was not the Devil itself, but rather the immense power that gave that fallen angel its nature. Two non-substantial powers, love and sin, were to purposefully face off. But how to make it possible? A special existential reality was needed for that to occur in and it was the human person who suited the requirements perfectly.

People are created in the image of God and are capable of nuanced expressions of love and sin. The human being is the only creature in the universe in whom those powers coexist with the capacity to discern good from evil. People can make wilful choices as is highlighted in the creation story of Genesis. The wrong choice by a person, the first Adam, allowed sin to infiltrate the earth foreshadowing that it would be on earth where sin was to be expelled by means of another person, the last Adam (1Cor. 15:45). The battle between love and sin was to be fought in the world amongst its people.

So, the Son of God 'emptied himself, taking on the form of a servant (slave), being born in the likeness of men. And being found in human form he humbled himself and became obedient unto death, even death on the cross' (Phil. 2:7-8). A saviour was born and crucified to fight in a spiritual battle of cosmic consequences, so enormous that it will ever be beyond our comprehension. The personification of love, Jesus Christ, allowed that of evil, Satan, to attack and invade the Son, who absorbed this assault from sin in the power of love, never choosing otherwise, until sin was exhausted and it became fully subject to God.

This event reached into the Trinity and exposed it to deep suffering also. There would have been nothing harder for the Father than to disconnect from the Son, who *became* sin (2Cor. 5:21), and leave him to his plight.

Sin has no place within divine reality, God is incapable of being in relation with it, and thus the Son was left to fight alone. For that reason, while on the cross, Jesus asked why his Father had forsaken him (Mat. 27:46). It was a bottomless despair in a death which is not of this world.

The notion that the Godhead knows not what it is to suffer is wrong. When creation that finds it existence in the Son suffers, a fully relational God suffers. Jesus would have carried the experiences of suffering from his earthly life into the Trinity also. Lady Julian of Norwich explains that the Lord still suffers an unquenchable thirst today for creation to arrive at its final redemption. For it to be revealed in its glory and the Lord's suffering ends.

The legitimacy of sin as a power has been defeated and sin is now under God's control. By God's wisdom it remains operative in creation yet for a season. The victory of Christ is divine in nature and thus beyond space and time. It reaches into the past and the future. It guarantees that creation will not remain subject to its present condition without end. It makes possible that upon death all that has life will arrive in Paradise. 'Oh death where is your victory?' Apostle Paul exclaimed (1 Cor. 15:55). Most amazingly, the spirit of that new reality has already entered our present creation. God's ways are wonderful.

13

A Second Birth

The most important event ever in the history of creation happened on earth. When death strikes, a person's spirit goes back to God and the body disintegrates into the dust (Eccl. 12:7). The returning spirit carries an imprint of what that person has experienced on earth. The spirit is in a state contaminated by sin. Something never seen before with human death one day happened. On the cross Jesus disempowered sin completely and cleansed himself fully of its corruption. Consequently when dying, for the first time ever, a spirit appeared after death that solely existed in love and perfection. A pure and perfect spirit person without sin. It was in Jerusalem that this occurred and is known as the resurrection of Christ. It decided the future of all of creation and is remembered at Easter.

In response to this achievement by the Son, the Father clothed Jesus' spirit with a new type of body in which sin, and thus death, no longer could find a foothold. It was a divine act executed in a cave on earth. Jesus rose from the dead a new person of a kind not seen before. All through his redemptive suffering creation never ceased to exist in him. Neither did it so when he newly arrived outside the tomb asking Mary Magdalene not to touch him for as yet he had not presented himself to the Father (John 20:18). Jesus, now a new creation person, arrived before God in heaven, the first of a multitude to follow. God proceeded with a new creation that again would find its existence in the Son. With sin defeated that creation was to be perfect and everlasting.

The transformation of our present world was set in motion. Like a caterpillar that turns into a butterfly, there is no discontinuity between the current and the new creation for both hold together in Christ. Two creations presently co-exist in one Person as an integrated reality. Karl Rahner in his book of reflections *The Eternal Year* (1964) described it well. 'The new creation has already started, the new power of a transfigured earth is already being formed from the world's innermost heart.' One day God will do a great deed: the first creation will be no more and the second will last forever.

The creation story in Genesis tells us that when creating the human being God personally blew life into Adam, the first person (Gen. 2:7). Thus natural life began for the human race. During his walk in Israel Jesus explained to Nicodemus that to enter the kingdom of God however you had to be born not merely of a natural birth but also a spiritual one (John 3: 3-8). You would have to be born again. Jesus introduced the actual reality of it when meeting up with his disciples for the first time after his resurrection. The next phase of what being human could mean began. Similarly to God in Genesis, Jesus blew on his followers and said, 'Receive holy spirit' (John 20:22). They became born again of a new spirit and into a new reality.

In the original Greek text of the New Testament, when referring to the Holy Spirit in Person, the word 'the' appears. In all other instances, when just the spiritual dynamics that issue from the Holy Spirit are mentioned, this definite pronoun is missing. The Greek then reads as 'holy spirit' and it doesn't demand a capital H and S.

The idea of 'holy spirit' aligns with that of 'universal spirit'. Both issue from the Holy Spirit and their similarity is as such that in unison they can shape the human spirit. Being born again happened to the disciples of Jesus and since then to all who have invited the Lord into their lives. Believers are born into a New Creation.

14

A New Creation

Christians are endowed with a holy spirit. Consequently Apostle Paul declared that he no longer looks at believers as merely naturally born, but rather as people of special spiritual significance. Anyone born again in Christ is a new creation. Like Jesus, they belong to a future era even though still struggling in a world in strife. Paul enthused, 'the old has passed away and the new has come' (2Cor. 5:17).

The presence of holy spirit is bound to make a difference in a Christian's life, but how? It is a grace empowerment that sometimes is sensed but mostly works its influences in subtle ways. Those influences help in becoming a little more like Jesus both in identity and ability – more loving and better spiritually attuned. The fruit of the Spirit is an example of this.

The outcomes of grace empowerment depend on a desire for living closely to Jesus and learning from him.

His yoke is easy and his burden is light. Whatever spiritual growth Jesus is seeking for my life, it will be a manageable. It is sufficient to be an ordinary person in relation with Jesus and he is sure to guide my identity formation for the better.

Fruit grows slowly and that of the Spirit likewise. I must aim for 'love, joy, peace, patience, kindness, goodness, faithfulness, gentleness, self-control' (Gal. 5:22-23). Elsewhere Apostle Paul writes that love is patient, not jealous, boastful, arrogant or rude. Insists not on its own way, is irritable or resentful. It rejoices in what is right (1 Cor. 13:4-6). It makes for an intimidating list of relational qualities altogether and I will fall short. Jesus is not overly concerned with my failures but values my willingness to pursue those character traits of the Spirit. Over the years they will develop within me, some more than others, and I will feel a better person for it.

Apart from the nature of Christ, the new creation grace enablement facilitates human ability. Personal aptitudes are enhanced in subliminal ways. Apostle Paul mentioned gifts such as teaching, administration, giving, encouraging and others (Rom. 12:6-8) Also, he recognised gifts of a seemingly more distinctly spiritual nature. A Christian's awareness of these usually depends on denominational association. Gifts such as the ability to prophecy, to have wisdom or special insights, or an unusually strong faith. The gifts of healing the sick and, far less common, doing miracles. Then there is the ability available to all believers, if desired, of speaking in tongues (1Cor. 12:4-11).

I am familiar with these gifts; have seen the positives and the negatives. The spiritual realm is full of pitfalls and care is needed. The focus must remain on Jesus and the Holy Spirit. Charismatic styles of worship always enrich spiritual life. An overemphasis on spiritual gifts however is best avoided. Insight on what is truly of the Holy Spirit and what is driven by a believer's psychology will remain difficult.

Seeking the fruit of the Spirit is sufficient to well please the Lord. It is most important and comes first in new creation living. 'If I have not love, I am nothing' (1Cor. 13-2).

15

A Greater Reality

There is more between heaven and earth than might be imagined. It helps to be aware of the good while the bad must be avoided. The Greater Reality is a world of spirits and earthly influences in which angels and evil spirits are facing off. That is the impression given in Scripture. Today's Western world in its self-sufficiency and science oriented perspectives considers it an illusion. Modern knowledge of the psyche ascribes the idea of spirits manifesting in human behaviour as a dysfunction of the soul due to unresolved inner difficulties or mental illness. Such assessments may often be correct but are not always the whole truth. Psychology remains ignorant of external spiritual influences.

I am little interested in the Greater Realm, apart from that related to God, but feel it needs a mention. After all, the Bible takes it seriously and throughout mentions angels. When tempted in the desert by Satan, before his walk through Israel, Jesus was ministered to by angels (Mark 1:13). Jesus himself liberated people from evil spirits. Perhaps some of the pressures I feel in life may be due to negative spirits having a go at unsettling me. I am never sure and don't much care. I always focus on the Lord asking for help when faced with confusing emotions and difficult experiences whatever their origin. A little story from the times of the Desert Fathers (4th century) comes to mind. One such recluse had been wrestling with his demons all night finally turning to Jesus for help. He queried with the Lord why he had left him alone in his struggles for so long. Not so, Jesus replied, as soon as you asked for me, I came immediately. It makes a nice point about never waiting to get the Lord involved in anything.

A giant in the faith who took the Greater Realm seriously was Apostle Paul. He was either deluded or he knew something. This was a man who was taken up to the third heaven, into Paradise he called it, and saw things he was not allowed to discuss (2Cor. 12:3-4). Paul was a mystic and it shaped this theological understanding. He was the man who gave us the Gospel and suffered greatly in doing so. But he kept on going for he had seen something while in the spirit about Jesus and creation's future that needed telling around the world. In doing so he understood to be opposed by spiritual forces, but did not take his cue from that. Rather, it was the Holy Spirit who guided him where to go or not (Acts 16:6-10).

These days Christianity usually is not much involved with the realm of spirits. Not so in the Middle Ages when the fear of demons was very real and the church used this dread to further its significance as a safe haven. When the Enlightenment arrived that all changed and just as well. But remaining unawares that our world is the theatre in which good and evil are spiritually at war is short-sighted. There are powerful dynamics in play that influence global affairs.

In the creation story of Genesis, the snake-like Tempter is deceiving Adam and Eve with drastic consequences. Temptations towards the negative are ever active in life. Paul encouraged believers to be strong in the Lord for spiritual influence, which he called the wiles of the devil, might be active. 'For we are not contending against flesh and blood, but against principalities, against the powers, against the world rulers of this present darkness, against the spiritual host of wickedness in heavenly places' (Eph. 6:12).

Paul would have encountered this in proclaiming the Gospel. He even considered false teaching about God to be influenced by elemental spirits of the universe (Col. 2:20-23). However all this is interpreted, to the church it was a warning about religious practices and life in general – the individual and societal. He advised believers to be alert and stand strong in their faith, as taught by him.

16

Standing Strong

The human spirit connects to a greater spiritual reality in which God's influences and those of sin are active. People are subject to dynamics either for good or evil. The Lord's Prayer recognises it and contains the well-known verse, 'Lead us not into temptation, but deliver us from evil (or the evil one)' (Mat. 6:13). The challenges of living responsibly and making the right choices are ever present.

Apostle Paul encourages to push back hard against negative temptations and to stand strong with the Lord's mighty help (Eph. 6:10-17). He uses the image of putting on an armour like that of Roman soldiers. How much temptations originate from within my soul or are also derived from outside spiritual influences is difficult to know. Nor does it matter much. My response to the challenge does not change. I must master temptation as God so clearly told Cain. Paul's suggestion of a spiritual armour is helpful towards psycho-spiritual wellbeing.

A Roman armour does not protect a soldier's back and as a Christian I do well in facing difficulties head on. It is the girdle that keeps the body armour together and Paul suggests: *Gird your loins with truth.* Jesus said, 'I am the way, the truth and the life' (John 14:6). Truth is the Gospel and seeking to live out the nature of Christ. Jesus told the Samaritan women that those who worship God must do so in spirit and in truth. *Put on the breastplate of righteousness.* I must be convinced of my worth in God and shun self-righteousness. Any person who questions my worth or doubts it, even myself, I will not listen to. *Feet shod with the gospel of peace.* The road may be rough at times but I will seek harmony with all where possible and offer respect. Good relating is key to a truly Christian life. *Take up the shield of faith to quench the flaming darts of the evil one.* Faith is an act of my spirit supported by my mind. I will not be shaken in what I believe to be true about my Lord. I am divinely loved by him and worthy. *Put on the helmet of salvation.* Doubts will arise occasionally about matters pertaining to God and I will not allow those to linger. Rather, my mind will treasure the many good things promised to me in Jesus every day. *Use the sword of the Spirit, which is the word of God.* There is spiritual power in what God's Word tells me about myself as a Christian. In my mind and in prayer I can use that affirmatively in challenging circumstances or for regularly strengthening my spirit.

These comments made about the armour of God are a guide, brief but helpful to every day. The picture Paul paints describes the Christian life well. As mentioned, whether the dynamics of my soul come from within myself or are at times orchestrated by outside spiritual influence, I care little about. Paul's armour is relevant rain or shine. I walk in step with the best general ever to be found, the Lord Jesus, and may stand strong whatever the circumstances.

17

Scripture

The Bible is a book about God and people. Over time God and the divine plan became better understood while the true nature of God was revealed in its fullness by Jesus Christ. The biblical accounts are historical containing narrative, poetry, wisdom literature, prophecy and the gospel. The Bible is meant to inspire, but also can sow confusion and lead to disputes. Wars have been fought about disagreement regarding its interpretation; people have been persecuted and burned at the stake by the Church for matters of belief that these days are common and uncontested. Religion has these tendencies and not because of God but because of human nature; when what God is like is not well understood or simply ignored.

The problem arose early in the days of Israel. God was guiding the nation in taking a promised land and was thought by Israel to be a warrior God. A deity that could instruct to kill women and children. It took a long time before God's true nature became better known.

There are inconsistencies in the Bible and the culture of its writers is recognisable in the text. Often Scripture is not a first-hand account and has been written from memory, historical records and generally known age-old stories. Modern scholarship, with the help of new source material discovered recently, is able to contextualise biblical texts better now than before.

Differences of opinion have always been around. An example is the content of the Bible itself in which the Catholic version has more books that the Protestant one. While Martin Luther felt free to suggest that the letter of James should never have been included and preferably Revelation not either.

The Jewish faith has no problem with arguing about the Old Testament and related texts and have done so ever since they were written. Not so Christianity where some these days hold that every word has been dictated by the Holy Spirit, is accurate to the point, and should not be meddled with. Historically it is a recent development that raises some questions. The obvious one that of the language in which the Bible is being read.

Scriptures original languages cannot be accurately translated without adaptation. It is unavoidable. While translations between them will offer different nuances of feeling and sometimes even understandings of the same verses. Add to that the possibility of varied interpretation of a verse in one language and God's Word becomes far from homogenous.

The Bible is not a textbook set in stone but a book that offers a spectrum of instructions and insights. It stirs the spirit, engages the intellect and speaks to the heart. Surely, God's spirit has been involved in the writing. Its revelations, wisdom and linguistic expressions present as inspired and are of the highest standard.

Believers find codes and patterns in the Bible, which they think predict the world's future including the return of Christ, even though Jesus himself admitted not to know the day – only his Father does.

What matter most of all is the primary message of God: the full story of creation, Jesus and the gospel. The Bible clearly reveals it. I have secondary interests and have written some books on those but always with God in mind, faith seeking understanding; how God, the giver of love and life, could be relevant in whatever situation we find ourselves in, whether simply being alive, studying philosophy or the sciences.

I would rather not enter into disputes about biblical issues and seek to respect different points of view. My insights are held firmly but not absolutely so. Reading

Scripture I may face 'unknowing' when something defies my understanding.

The Bible is a fascinating book that can become a stumbling block, or a bone of contention even, between people individually and between groups. Boundaries to its interpretation are necessary, which is called orthodoxy. Within it conceptual creativity remains possible perhaps stretching those boundaries a little in order to move understanding forward. It is how knowledge progresses.

A smart way in reading God's Word is to avoid becoming stuck with a problematic text unless making a study of it. Rather, follow Apostle John's encouragement to abide in Jesus who has anointed every believer to know the wheat from the tares. John strongly suggests that, 'you have no need that anyone teach you; as his anointing teaches you about everything…' (1John 2:27). It concerns being able to discern what Jesus and the Christian life is really about.

In moments that the Bible begins to inspire surely the anointing is active. It is then that Jesus who is the Word, and who was in the beginning before anything was created, speaks into the soul (John 1:1). The Bible is a wonderful book that needs relaxed reading with many moments of reflection.

18

Living Waters

In our frantic world a little peace is hard to find. Jesus invites me to learn from him and find some rest for my soul. It is an ever ongoing process. A focus on the Lord reminds me of what I am about and is distinctly helpful in facing the vagaries of daily life. The Lord always points towards what is important and conducive to my soul's wellbeing. It is a good approach in dealing with everyday concerns and the wisdom required for correct decisions, many of which will be of a practical nature. All of this is influenced by my disposition, which is a matter of spirit and relation. Getting things right helps towards harmony in situations and towards peace of mind.

My walk with Jesus needs to remain vibrant. When the edge comes off, life feels less anchored and more in flux. Therefore, I make sure to spend time with the Lord and do so in two ways. The first is keeping the Lord in the back of the mind all through the day. The second involves private time in a quiet place – with varied results.

In those times of reflection I may be restless and find it hard to settle down, feeling that connecting with the Lord isn't happening, and I give up. I am coming up short but then, I'm only human. Jesus appreciates my effort all the same. Usually it takes a few minutes to focus my spirit. I apply my mind towards the Lord without hurry and will find my spiritual perception sharpening. Verbal prayers are of value, but in finding rest the sound of my voice is distractive, as is the effort needed for such prayers. I will remain silent and reflective. 'Be still and know that I am God' (Psalm 46:10).

Verbal prayer has its place when problems arrive. Talking to the Lord about important issues unburdens the heart. Ending those prayers with a brief expression of worship is good practice. Be confident and trust that the Lord has heard you immediately. Make sure that the nature of any request aligns with the nature of God – towards the good and wholesome, not egocentric and seeking recompense.

Mostly though I relate to the Lord in contemplation; in unhurried reflection that simply enjoys his presence. When seeking insight into a matter the Lord may drop an idea into my mind which has happened countless times. Often, I try to think as little as possible making sure that thoughts I do have will remain towards the Lord. In that manner I refresh my spirit, even though not always does it feel that way.

Come and walk with me, Jesus says. When in worship sometimes a church congregation may reach out with 'Jesus come!' Though the idea is clear enough and surely of value, the invitation actually has it back to front. Jesus is ever present and lives in us. The right call would be, 'Lord, our hearts are coming!' It is the best call a Christian can make.

Besides inviting the people in Israel to learn from him, there was another significant moment at which Jesus shouted, 'Come unto me!' It happened during a week-long religious feast, on the last and most important day. At the high point of the Feast of Tabernacles, when the waters of ablution were poured out over the altar, Jesus called out, 'If any one thirst, let him come to me and drink … Out of his (her) heart shall flow rivers of living water' (John 7:37-38). Those waters are a gift of the Spirit and a miracle waiting to happen in every Christian. When walking intimately with God such living water is bound to flow forth from those who love the Lord and to the benefit of many. Such a Christian is always a good person to be with – an uplifting presence.

19

Heaven

What may be said about the world's eternal destination? Jesus told the criminal who hung crucified next to him, 'today you will be with me in Paradise' (Luke 23:39-44). Simply, because the man declared the Lord to be without guilt and asked to be remembered when Jesus would enter into his kingdom The Bible refers to this kingdom as that of God, or of heaven.

Apostle Paul writes that, 'What no eye has seen, nor ear heard, nor heart of man conceived, what God has prepared for those who love him, God has revealed to us through the Spirit' (1Cor. 2:9-10). Paul was referring to the arrival of a new spiritual reality through Jesus that now could be entered into by believers. What has been prepared for those who love God is inconceivable, in our days already, with the mystery of a second spiritual birth. And surely also regarding what the future in heaven is to be like. It will be beyond imagination.

Heaven is incredible, but familiar all the same, with

the presence of people of a new creation kind. Nature, creatures and vegetation will likewise be transformed and recognisable, I suggest. Creation is renewed in Christ, and not discarded with God starting wholly afresh. There is a continuity from the old to the new. It will be amazing.

The question often asked is what will happen when I die? Around the world answers vary from nothing, to coming back one day, or going to a better place. The latter is the sure hope of heaven that Christians have. Stories exist of ill people who felt to have visited heaven before coming back into consciousness. Accounts vary, but there is a consistency in the experience of how kind the Lord is and how nice is the place where they have been. None of the accounts could possibly be of the 'no eye has seen' kind that Apostle Paul suggests. The sense of heaven though invariably was pleasant.

Scripture explains that upon death my body will return to the dust and my spirit goes to God (Eccl. 12:7). I hold that the shape of my spirit will resemble my body for how else would I be recognisable? During my time on earth the history of my life in all its aspects will have been recorded in my spirit. Thus upon death I will remain the person that I am. My soul awareness, which results from my body and spirit interacting, will cease to be as I have departed from my body. I will now be aware in spirit only.

Every person facing the 'Pearly Gates' will be assessed in accordance with the life lived. In this process Apostle Paul thought a person's conscience to be key (Rom. 2:15-16). The light of Love will shine and show up the shadows of a life lived on earth. In my book *The Primacy of Love* I have a chapter called, 'Love's Day in Court', which I would like to quote from.

> In a court of love the benchmark is love. Not only with regard to the accused, but first of all for the court itself; it will have to dispense justice in love. Love seeks to embrace, to forgive and restore. But it will call a spade a spade. It seeks to forgive, but it will not overlook. No-one is expected to be perfect, far from it, and Love does not have a pointing finger, rather open arms of acceptance. Mistakes are soon covered by love where possible. ... God will be gracious (page 170).

In heaven a person's spirit is cleansed of the marks of sin and it makes receiving a new body possible. Good will be rewarded and evil purged. A transformation into the new awaits all of creation. *All* shall be well, Julian of Norwich saw so clearly. But when she questioned the Lord how that could be with church teaching condemning many to hell, he answered her just this: 'What is impossible to you is not impossible to me … I shall make everything well' (Chap. 32).

In the new reality to come sin will not have managed to steal anything created by God away from Jesus Christ in whom it all holds together. The Son's total victory over sin, past present and future, makes that a certainty. It is a mystery – but a beautiful one. Heaven awaits!

20

Meaning

The idea of walking with God suggests a steady pace that is not overly demanding. The Christian life is not a sprint, neither a marathon with all the exhaustion that brings. The walk of life leads through all kinds of situations and opportunities and having a suitable mentor in personal development is a great advantage. There is no better than Jesus, who is always gentle and lowly in heart. Walking in partnership with him is both a joy and a privilege. It is life changing and distinctly meaningful.

Walking with God brings the best meaning into life. The idea of 'what is it all about?' often arises and is intrinsic to personhood. The ultimate meaning of creation rests with God, who one day will transform creation into an eternal Paradise. The meaning of life on earth is another matter. A singular statement will not sum it up and it involves values. Meaning is found by giving prominence to certain values over others, values that concern morality and also beliefs that I hold.

A nihilist decides there to be no significant value in life and thus no meaning. For others, life is just life and meaning is hardly considered. Some are well aware of the question of meaning but little interested. They prefer to live by values that come naturally to them.

Those who are intrigued by the meaning of life do best in considering their values and find those that are significant and profitable to self and others. For the real meaning of existence reflects the nature of God. Good values engender good living and thus meaning is found. Always, the true meaning of life is relational and is never discovered when taking a self-centred point of view. That is universally so. The Christian should know what the search for meaning involves for the Bible is clear on it. Love the Lord your God and your neighbour as yourself (Matt. 22:37-40).

What is wise and important in life is discovered over time by exposure to significant others and self-education. For a Christian that education is guided by Scripture and in taking seriously what God has revealed. Do it well and the satisfaction of living meaningfully looks after itself. The most precious meaning a believer will find is in the Lord personally. In knowing him meaning transcends worldly realities and becomes ultimately rounded – the earthly enveloped by the divine.

In his book *Contemplation is a World of Action,* Thomas Merton describes how love and value are closely related. With meaning deriving from value, at its best, meaning is an expression of love.

> Love is not a mere emotion or sentiment. It is the lucid and ardent response of the whole man to a value that is revealed to him as perfect, appropriate and urgent in the providential context of his own life.

Walking with God solves the question of meaning and leads into the liberty of Christ. It is a personal journey in which you wear your moccasins and I wear mine. But the nature of the journey will be the same for both of us: towards a deeper understanding of the Lord and psycho-spiritual wellbeing. Following Jesus brings wholeness and rest. As a fellow traveller, on 'that special way', I wish you well with much sunshine and sufficient shelter when it rains.

AgapeDeum

Other books by Michael J Spyker

Meeting Emma
An introduction to Christian Spirituality in which Emma learns from theologian Joe how to involve God's spirit in everyday living.

The Primacy of Love
How a theological understanding that creation is essentially an expression of God's love leads to a model that explains the dynamics of human relating based on the Trinity.

Julian's Windows
A contemporary love story that contextualises many teachings of medieval mystic Lady Julian of Norwich.

The Language of Love
A love story that encourages wisdom and wellbeing, and seeking an authentic relationship with Jesus Christ.

Science and Spirit
How science and spirit exist is relation and what that means to Christian understanding.

Oh My Soul!
The meaning of soul, the roots of its awareness, and how soul health is helped by a Christian understanding of the dynamics involved.

Drawings and Reflections
52 short reflections on Christian vibrancy with full-colour illustrations by Jeanne Spyker Hardy.

Living Well
The art of making the best of life relationally. Though based on Christian insights this little book is meant for everyone and avoids religious references.

I Am Willing
A story about miracles and more based on the ministry of Dean Knight, who authors this little book with the help of Michael Spyker.

Shalomat
An adventure in which two young people are being chased across Australia while seeking to fulfil a riddle that has global consequences. The story is based on ideas from spirituality and philosophy.

Available at agapedeum.com